THE MINI-MANUAL FOR BECOMING SUPER-AWESOME

YOUR KICK-START GUIDE TO AN EPIC LIFE

BY JOHN BEEDE

ISBN: 978-0-9765697-1-8

ABOUT THE AUTHOR

John Beede has climbed the tallest mountain on every continent and kitesurfed every ocean on earth.

He is a professional speaker and author who has delivered keynote speeches in Brazil, Mexico, New Zealand, Australia, China, the UK, Canada, and 48 US States.

For a free masterclass by the author, post your favorite line from this book on Instagram and tag @johnbeede.

If you would like to have John Beede deliver a rock-concert style motivational presentation at your next conference or other function, please contact:

1-800-CLIMB-ON
(1-800-254-6266)

www.johnbeede.com

@johnbeede on all social media.

THIS BOOK IS DEDICATED TO YOU

I wrote it so that when you're much older, you'll be one of those people with big 'ol laugh lines on your face and a sparkle in your eyes.

IT'S ALSO DEDICATED TO MY PARENTS

They're two of the most super-awesome humans I know.

FORWARD

This book's contents are sourced from monks in Nepal, caballeros in Argentina, and yodelers in the Swiss Alps (no, really). It's the 24 most useful pieces of advice that I've personally heard from US Senators, world-class self-help gurus, athletes, authors, and psychologists. They're all are represented here, as are philosophers, new and ancient, plus church, mosque, temple, and synagogue leaders.

My 'learning' of these ideas occurred as I traveled to 65 countries, kitesurfed every ocean, and climbed to the summit of the tallest mountain on of every continent. I paid for those adventures with businesses I built from scratch and either sold or operated and profited from while working remotely.

Throughout those expeditions, I was searching. Searching for *who* to be. I was asking, "how can a person live their best life?"

Well, my *actual* question, being a kitesurfer and a climber, was, "what makes a person super-awesome?"

Here's where it took an unexpected turn: several tragedies and close calls showed me, up close and personal, how short and precious life can be. The surprising result was that I became hyper-aware of how temporary we are. That's when I started asking the "super-awesome" question with a passionate desire to synthesize what I learned.

I kept thinking, this thing we have called life?! It's short! I wanna make the most of it! HOW DO I DO THAT?

This book is the answer I came to. This is the best stuff I've learned. It's how I strive to live, each day. I invite you to try these ideas on for size, and I hope they help you to live out a super-awesome life adventure of your own.

- *JB*

PART I

SUPER-AWESOME FOUNDATIONS

1 | SEEK DEEP JOY

"When you do things from your soul, you feel a river moving in you, a joy."

-RUMI

You will become super-awesome when you design a lifestyle that gives you a sense of deep, soul-penetrating joy.

That's it! In that single sentence lies the entire answer to "how can I become super awesome?" The rest of this mini-manual, therefore, is your guide to making it happen. Together, we're going to craft you a sense of joy that's so authentic and complete that you will feel like an unstoppable rock-star at life.

When you have joy that feels like it's superseded the laws of physics and has connected you with the people, land, and Creator alike, you'll have become a person who is irresistibly attractive to others. They'll think you're super awesome. Why? Because you will BE super-awesome. You'll be authentic, true to you. Your best personality will be on display. Not for the sake of impressing, mind you, but rather, you will simply BE impressive.

When life throws you hardships, difficulties, and sorrows (and it will), you will blatantly and audaciously find a way to let your inner light shine. Because of that, others will *just know* that you're super-awesome.

Let me say, right up front, that being super-awesome isn't about becoming a carbon-copy of another person. It's not about accomplishing major feats, setting world records, having a bunch of online followers, or impressing people with your wit on Twitter. It's not about salaries, grades, or possessions.

Pursuing those things as ends in themselves is like eating fast-food. You'll feel full, maybe even bloated, but oddly, you'll still feel hungry and always craving more.

Of course, you may very well *want* to take on the characteristics of other people. You may choose to follow success formulas, accomplish bloody amazing feats, generate an eye-popping salary, ace your exams, and own some flashy toys. I absolutely encourage you pursue and get those things... in the right context.

However, I implore you to never make these things your journey's final destination.

Instead, think of your accomplishments as though they are mile-markers along the path to deep joy. Make finding deep joy your ultimate goal and you will be well on your way towards being totally super-awesome.

That's what this book is about. Finding deep joy WHILE you crush it at all the other stuff.

Let's dive in.

2 | START FRESH

"Our sorrows and wounds are only healed when we touch them with compassion."

- BUDDHA

I'm not always great at the stuff in this book. In fact, I frequently crash and burn when trying.

But I try, which is all any of us can actually do. This stuff is my aim.

I'm not standing here saying, "look how super awesome I am! Be like me!" No. Far from that. I've failed at all of them at different times.

Sometimes I succeed at one or another, and I don't think I've ever been great at every one of them, especially not all at once.

If you're human, you'll be the same. Perfection is not expected.

But failure can feel EXHAUSTING.

Fortunately, when it doesn't go as planned, there is a magic key to making a comeback with fresh energy.

That key is self-forgiveness.

Please trust me when I say I'd have once barfed in my mouth if I ever read that in chapter two of a book.

If you're rolling your eyes like I once would have, then do it with this in mind:

If you beat yourself up every time you don't live up to a standard – from this book or anywhere else – you will develop a habit of being self-critical. In fact, even as you succeed, you'll be more focused on your mistakes than your gains. This results in feeling like a constant failure.

Not exactly helpful when it comes to experiencing deep joy.

That's why, when something goes wrong along the way, or if you've made a mistake and you've done all you can do to make it right, you must learn to forgive yourself. Otherwise, you'll be like a hiker who picks up every stone you trip on.

Before you know it, you'll be carrying around a lot of weight.

Each individual stone may not feel *that* heavy, but you'll soon be slowed. And eventually, stopped in your tracks.

If you find yourself stuck for too long under the weights of, "I've lost my love," or "I've lost my wealth," or "I've lost my health," just decide to drop those bitter stones, no matter who's at fault. There was a time when you didn't have these things. They were a gift or a reward given to you. Now, they're gone. You haven't lost them, they've just been returned to where they came.

The only way to start fresh, when pursuing anything new (especially deep joy!) is to forgive yourself when you inevitably don't live up to the heightened standards you've set for yourself.

Self-forgiveness is the secret-sauce for renewed passion and mental energy.

We grow by our mistakes, and without self-forgiveness, you'll be ironically stuck under the weight of those very mistakes, never able to reach your destination.

The depth of your joy is directly limited by your capacity for self-compassion. Said differently: deep joy is impossible if you're not kind to yourself.

And you know? While you're at it, get good at forgiving others, too. Don't carry the stones of resentment around either. Why are you carrying around the stones that others put into your backpack?

You don't forgive because someone else deserves it, you forgive because you deserve to be free of that weight.

Same goes for self-forgiveness.

Drop the weight. Forgive. Start fresh. And move on.

3 | SHIFT YOUR MIND'S FOCUS

"I don't care how much power, brilliance or energy you have, if you don't harness it, and focus it on a specific target, and hold it there, you're never going to accomplish as much as your ability warrants."

-ZIG ZIGLAR

There is no quality that any great maker of history possessed that you can't cultivate and develop as well.

Earth's greatest achievers -- political leaders, warriors, world-class athletes, billionaires, humanitarians, celebrities, great orators, scientists, philosophers, and theorists alike, were all (here's a real shocker) human. So are you (duh).

Unless you're a wackadoodle conspiracy theorist, this is not news to you.

While that was a big build-up to an obvious statement, the important conclusion seems to be lost on many people is…

If they were able to do what they accomplished, as regular humans, then YOU, TOO, can accomplish what they accomplished… and possibly even take it to the next level.

A common reactionary response to that concept is some variety of lame or invalid excuse. "I'm not smart enough, strong enough, tall enough, tough enough, blah, blah, blah. I'm not the right gender, race, religion, sexuality, don't have the right education, don't have the training, certification, finances, people skills, blah freaking blah."

Yes, genetics are a factor in the most extreme cases, but DNA isn't the most limiting factor for top-level performance. All those other things I mentioned? You're right. They're important. But they aren't required to get started -- or even to perform exceedingly well and push the limits -- any more it was required for Ben Franklin to have a degree in electrical engineering before he discovered electricity.

Now, before you start sticking paperclips into electrical sockets and writing a Constitution, understand what I'm saying: the *most* limiting factors towards your success are your own excuses about why YOU think you can't or won't succeed.

Is other stuff important? Yes. Absolutely. Is there more to success than just having a great mindset? You bet. But it IS your mindset, above all, that is the greatest influencing factor.

Certifications, trainings, and education are all massively important and can help you shortcut your way to success. Oftentimes those are necessary steps along the way. But the most important starting place is to…

Shift your mind's focus.

Start focusing on what you CAN do instead of what limitations you have

Start believing that because other humans, like you, made it as far as they did, that you, too, can succeed.

That's an easy thing to say but a tricky thing to do. Let's be honest: will you suddenly start thinking like the Dalai Llama or Mother Theresa by the end of this chapter?

Probably not.

But you *can* take a step in that direction.

Here's how: the easiest way to shift your mindset is to choose three of your personal heroes and write down their admirable qualities. Define -- on paper -- what makes you admire them.

Who are they and why are they your heroes? Maybe someone from history? A family member? Someone you work for? A political or sports figure?

Once you figure out who they are, identify those traits. And do it for all three! What made them so super-awesome, by your definition, that they became your heroes? Write those qualities down.

OK, so now you have this list of traits that you admire, and examples of people who are great at executing the characteristics that you admire…

Congratulations! Now, whenever you're stuck, all you have to do is ask yourself, "How would any ONE of my heroes act in this situation that I'm in right now, were they in my shoes?"

If those people are heroic to you, then doing what they would do in your shoes is how you, too, can be heroic! For whatever you're going through, pick the most appropriate hero for your situation and ask yourself how they'd handle it. Which of their traits do you need to embody in order to overcome?

See what you're doing? You're modeling your very own definition of greatness. You're calling on their wisdom, asking for their help as you act out their virtues – which are, in fact, your virtues.

You would be correct in assuming that in order to do this well, you need to know a lot about your heroes. So learn! How did they become who they are? How did they train? What did they study? Who were their coaches and mentors? What were their habits?

Take action on what you discover and you will get a similar outcome as those heroes of yours. That's how you shift your own mindset... by trying on the mindsets of others! If they did what they did, then SO CAN YOU by doing the same processes that they've already proven to work!

You can't get to an increased level of performance with the same poor level of thinking that's got you stuck. That's not meant to be derogatory or insulting, it's just reality. Our thinking helps us get to a certain level, but then we have to change it if we want to progress.

That's why you've got to shift your thoughts if you want to change your life to make it super-awesome.

Boo-ya! Keep it up, you hero, you! Flip that page to the next chapter and let's keep up the momentum. You're crushing it, after all. Why stop now?

4 | VALUE GROWTH

"One can choose to go back toward safety or forward toward growth. Growth must be chosen again and again; fear must be overcome again and again."

– ABRAHAM MASLOW

Only three things are certain in life. 1) You will be born. 2) You will grow. 3) You will die.

That's the entire list of what we know for sure.

Given those certainties, consider where your current situation fits in on the list:

You're already here. And you're not dead yet. So you are here to 'grow.' In fact, that's the only thing you can do, right now, that is 100% certain.

An Everest climber arrived at the legendary mountain's summit after seven weeks of effort. She trekked through remote villages, crossed massive ice crevasses, hauled gear up and down the mountain at sub-zero temperatures, all while gasping for air.

This epic battle culminated in fifteen minutes of celebration atop that ice-covered Himalayan peak.

No plant can grow at that elevation. No creature can make its home in those conditions. After a few minutes of enjoying the view, celebrating, and snapping some photos, she shivered in the wind, gripped her ice axe, and turned around. After another week, she safely made it home. There, she told her family and friends that those fifteen minutes were worth every second of the eight weeks of struggle it took her to reach the top.

She said her life was changed.

You'd be wise to think, "cool story, but how does someone's life get changed in fifteen minutes?"

It doesn't. Reaching the summit is never the true goal. Those 15 minutes at the summit are just the icing on the cake compared to the growth and self-discovery that takes place on the journey to the top.

The summit is always optional. Growth and self-improvement are mandatory results of all epic journeys.

Whether our mountaineering heroine broke her leg at base camp and quit -- or made the summit – doesn't make a difference to anyone but her.

Not a soul!

The only thing that will impact others is who she became during her experience.

What about you?

Whatever mountain you attempt, and whether you summit or plummet, it will be considered a failure by our joy-seeking standards unless you grow into a better, more compassionate, kinder human as a result of you experience.

When climbing towards your summits, don't get too focused on forcing the end-result you imagine. In life, you should not count on reaching every summit you set out to 'conquer' or to accomplish every single thing on your bucket list. No climber nor human has a 100% success rate (unless they're liars or inexperienced). That's not how life works.

In fact, believing that success means stabbing your ice-axe into the summit… is childish. Success is not about conquering.

Instead, shift your focus onto growing into an amazing person *while* you pursue your life's metaphorical summits.

That approach to live has a name, in fact. It's called "Kai-Zen."

Huh?

That's what Japanese Samurai Warriors called their practice of "constant, never-ending, self-improvement." Nowadays, the principle still remains in Japanese business. THAT, my friend, is success. Practicing Kai-Zen means you've committed to growth.

If you commit to Kai-Zen, then not only will you be growing (the only certain purpose we have in this life), but you'll also become super-awesome.

I believe in you. You're a warrior. You've got this. Focus on growth… and keep it up.

5 | PLAY

"We don't stop playing because we grow old; we grow old because we stop playing."

-GEORGE BERNARD SHAW

Because growth is your new top priority, it only makes sense that you should get really, really good at it.

The two best ways to supercharge your rate of growth in any pursuit are to:

1. Love your inner idiot.

   and

2. Crave skill like food.

Boom. Those two steps are how to supercharge your rate of growth (with growth being your life's purpose… and pursuing your life purpose being how you achieve deep joy… and having deep joy being your metric for becoming super awesome).

Bam. Now that we've established the 'how,' let's expand on each of those two steps.

We'll start with "love your inner idiot."

You know that awkward, weird, horribly uncomfortable feeling when you decide to try something new, but you're painfully fearful that you look like a complete moron because you know you don't actually know what you're doing? I'm talking about those times when you're just making it up as you go and desperately hope that nobody else can see that you don't *actually* know what you're doing…

Yeah, that.

Learn to LOVE that feeling.

I call it the 'idiot phase.' And seriously? Welcome that inner fool with open arms.

I get it. That's strange advice. After all, why would I tell you to accept your inner moron whilst teaching you to become super-awesome?

I'm so glad you asked!

Here's the answer:

Kids (aka super-awesome young humans) have the capacity to learn and grow at a faster rate than you or I… BECAUSE they're not fully conscious of their own inner critics.

Each of our inner critics is hyper-paranoid, overly sensitive, and sometimes, totally unfounded. In fact, this inner critic has a nasty trick. It convinces you to unfairly assign it's criticism to other people. This way, your own criticism about yourself goes undetected, as you're tricked into believing that others are the ones doing the judging (meanwhile, everyone else is doing the same thing in their own heads, criticizing themselves and unfairly assigning the voice).

When our inner critics hack us down from their hiding places, the less we're willing to take risks. That means, we'll make fewer mistakes. But we only learn from our mistakes, which means that we have less material to learn from, so our growth comes to a grinding halt.

All because of that little tyrant in our minds who hides behind unfounded paranoias about what others might be thinking.

That's why I say, "be willing to fall flat on your face." In fact, be excited to do it! Learn to laugh when you make mistakes. *Hey! That was fun! And wasn't as bad as I thought!* When things are new and awkward and you feel like you're an idiot at the task at hand, learn to LOVE those moments!

Why?

Because the only way to handle these moments is to treat them like a child. It's to become like the best part of who you were, when you were a super-awesome young human kid.

There's a super-fancy name for what I'm talking about. In fact, many adults can't even pronounce this bizarre thing without cringing a bit, believing it comes with a lack a productivity... and my word, forget about them actually DOING this thing I'm referring to.

It's this:

PLAY.

Yeah. P-L-A-Y.

Play.

Play is how you supercharge your rate of growth. Play is where you have the freedom to make errors. Only… in play, errors aren't considered mistakes. Instead, they're just gleeful little moments that teach cause and effect with no judgements attached.

Play is exploration and discovery. When unexpected things happen as a result of our actions, we freaking crack up in laughter! Play is when our errors aren't hated or judged, but they are just plain… FUN!

No. Strings. Attached.

Okay, so that's how you get your own mind in check. But what about others? It's not like you can force them to read this book, right?

Well, authentic play is when your adult voice tells you that other people think you're being an idiot, or that you don't know what you're doing, or that you look foolish… when in fact, you're just re-connecting with your inner child.

And honestly… when was the last time you let yourself just *have* fun? Like, when was the last time that you OWNED having fun and the thought of adulting didn't even enter your mind…?

I'm talking about the tickle-wars variety of fun, where there are no winners nor losers, no objectives nor failures. The kind where you're experiencing deep joy, based on what you're doing, in this very moment. I'm talking about the real definition of being free: open-hearted, non-judgmental PLAY.

If you want to supercharge your growth, make a dedicated effort to bring play to as many areas of your work, your workouts, your family, your friendships, your EVERYTHING. In fact, introducing more play to each domain of your life is how you become unstuck when you're in a rut and how you blast off to the next level when your progress has hit a plateau.

It's kind of like this: if you ever learn to partner dance, you will start out terrible. You'll stub your own toes and your partners' toes. It's a given. Enjoy the awkwardness and embrace it. That is what will help you to progress faster than otherwise.

Do young kids worry about what they look like when they dance? No. Do they try to stay on beat? No. Do they wonder if they're doing it right or if they suck at it? No. They dance when it feels good and they play in their dance, and figure it out as they go. That's precisely why they learn faster than we do (that's also part of why kids learn languages faster than adults).

Seriously, whenever facing a new challenge and you make a mistake, crack up laughing at how bad you are!

And here's the magic: *every moment* in life presents a new challenge. You'll accidentally step on toes and stub your own. You might even break your own toe, like I did when I started dancing (no, seriously. I broke it).

Laugh and enjoy it, knowing that you're exactly where you're meant to be: you are growing and learning.

And honestly, what kinda Scrooge McDuck curmudgeon doesn't want to play and have fun? In your deepest heart – and think back to when you were a kid on this one – do you honesty want to be that guy?

I'm going to assume the answer is a big 'ol 'hayullll no.' So play like you were a kid again. Whenever you can. After all, in every moment, we are all in the "sandbox" in some form or another, right? We're all just trying to figure this stuff out.

Part I of supercharging your growth is to play. Part II is in the next chapter. Keep the momentum going!

6 | VORACIOUSLY EDUCATE YOURSELF

"I'm still learning."

- MICHELANGELO

OK, so you've embraced the idiot phase and started to integrate play into everything you do. What's next? The second key to supercharge your growth is to voraciously educate yourself.

Here's the deal: A lot of people have already done what you want to do (or, at least are closer to it, right now, than you are).

That's great news, because many of them have spent hours and days and years putting their knowledge out there for you to learn from their experiences.

Bottom line? Take online courses. Read books with the passion of a banshee. Go to seminars. Listen to podcasts. Devour those how-to YouTube videos. Hire coaches.

You can short-cut your way to where you want to end up by piggybacking on the life-works of those who have already made mistakes... which means that you don't have to!

Study those who have 'figured it out.' Ask for help from those who can pinpoint what you're doing right and wrong. Ask how they overcame their 'sticking points' and got past their plateaus when they were at your level.

Do this, and you will progress with incredible speed.

And... just for a moment, onsider the real value of the information contained in a non-fiction book. Maybe that sounds boring, but really think about this: a person spends months, oftentimes years, organizing, synthesizing, and sharing their expertise onto those pages.

And the fact that you can acquire their life-knowledge for the same price of a mediocre lunch?! ... That's an incredible deal!

So, tatter up your books with notes and highlighting and dog ears. As your literature falls apart, your life will come together.

Your two steps to supercharge your growth are to 1) love your inner idiot in the form of play and 2) crave skill like it's food, in the form of voraciously educating yourself.

7 | FIND YOUR TALENT-PASSION INTERSECT

"Nothing is as important as passion. No matter what you want to do with your life, be passionate."

- JON BON JOVI

What are you really good at?

Those are your skills. They're also called, "talents." Nothing new here, moving right along…

Next, what do you lie awake dreaming about and what would you do for work *even if you had to pay* in order to do it?

Those are your passions.

Now, I'd like to ask you both of those two questions together, as one.

Like this: what *could you* become really good at that you also *want to* become really good at?

Your answer is the sweet spot for living.

The place where your skills and your passions overlap is where you'll discover your 'role' in life.

Most people never find that level of confidence in their life purpose. So pinpoint that crossroad for YOU and get both excited and grateful. You're now able to use your talent as your map and passion as your compass. Used together they'll accurately chart your life course, giving you a sense of meaning, significance, and ultimately, happiness.

If your talent-passion intersect doesn't make you a major celebrity or revered public figure, don't worry about it. Most people with fame aren't filled with deep joy anyway (and therefore, are not actually super-awesome).

Sure, aligning with your authentic talent-passion intersect *could* very well make you into a recognized public figure, but heed this warning: neither the pursuit nor the attainment of celebrity or leadership roles are enough to create deep joy.

Instead of pursuing fame, simply aspire to frequently 'check in' with the intersecting points of your talents and your passions. Doing this will give you the confidence to 'stay the course' without being distracted by shiny objects or tempting side-quests (ahem… that that's exactly what fame is).

Yet also know that it's a GOOD thing to adjust course as your talents and passions evolve. Your life purpose today is not the same as when you were 9 years old. Obvious, right? Well, it should be… but how many people are still pursuing the dreams of their 15 year old self when they are 25? Or their 29 year old self when they are 52? Or their 63 year old self when, god bless 'em, they're 106?

It's a mistake to chase the purpose of your younger self.

Who are you today? What's your talent-passion intersect in this moment, now?

That's where you belong.

8 | SOLVE THE ALMOST IMPOSSIBLE

"Each of us should have his or her own Everest—a testing place in any endeavor where the goal is almost, but not quite, beyond reach...

A life lived in this way is infinitely fulfilling."

- DR. KENNETH KAMLER

Most of us don't like 'goals.' I know this because my previous book was all about goals. What I learned, is that instead, we get more passionate about solving puzzles and fixing problems.

Here's how that matters to you: if you want to do some stuff with your life that's damn impressive and makes a difference in people's lives, make your goals into problems that you are desperate to solve.

More effective than setting some arbitrary goal that doesn't emotionally charge you up is to make your goals 'just beyond reach.'

What I mean by that, is to focus your efforts on solving problems that feel are *almost* impossible. Yet, the *almost* part of that nearly irritates you, because you know that there's a glimmer of hope that the puzzle can be solved. Deep down, you have a sliver of belief that you could solve that problem or accomplish that nearly impossible thing.

That's how I climbed Mt. Everest.

No, really.

I've got short, bowlegged legs. I'm round and don't have the physique of a mountaineer. I can't move as quickly as most accomplished climbers. Worst of all, I get pulmonary edema at high altitude, a potentially lethal condition where your lungs fill with fluid.

Not a great resumé for a guy who's going to high altitude.

But I also recognized that I fight like a bulldog. I bite and don't let go. I've got endurance, and I don't quit. I can take a lot of punches. That's what gave me a sliver of hope that I could maybe succeed.

So I shifted my mindset about having a 'goal' to climb earth's tallest mountain and instead made it into an almost impossible problem to solve: "what would it take for a naturally chubby, bowlegged, grunty guy like me, with lung problems, to reach 29,035 feet above sea level?"

Do you see how my goal got converted from a boring statement (I want to climb Mount Everest) into a burning question?

The minute I made that shift is when my passion and energy for the project took off to an unrecognizable level.

You can do the same thing with the massive mountains in your life.

When setting a goal, The formula is quite simple.

Start by asking yourself what's just beyond your mind's false ceiling about what you're capable of and what's possible for you. 'Feel out' your self-imposed limits. What do you think your disadvantages are?

Next, consider your talents and passions. These are your slivers of hope that maybe you could succeed.

Like this: "How would a person with limitations like mine accomplish this super-awesome thing?"

Boom.

You've set your goal just a little bit above your mind's false ceiling and your formula for success is in the form of a question. A puzzle. A problem to solve.

The slightly irksome and satisfying nature of puzzles and problem-solving is what gives us the endurance to succeed. It will be the same with cracking your false ceiling of capability.

Set the goal too lofty and you'll become intimidated and discouraged. Set the goal too low and you'll never feel challenged or motivated. Yet if you set your goals 'just beyond reach,' in that thin atmosphere of the 'almost impossible,' you'll discover the perfect balance of challenge and possibility. Together, those forces will work in tandem to keep you moving forward with unstoppable resolve.

What happens next is akin to magic. Your brain will start working in the background solve the puzzle you've presented to it.

Dr. Kenneth Kamler, the guy whose quote leads this chapter, explains it like this:

"When you take on a great challenge and persevere, you discover that your abilities are more than you ever imagined, enabling you at times to accomplish the 'impossible.'"

He's saying what I'm also trying to tell you: you will discover what you're really made of when you focus on solving the almost impossible.

OK, you're up: decide what that almost impossible thing is for you and write it down, in the form of a puzzle. An irksome question for your brain to start solving.

Having written goals is a given. If you don't have a bucket list, make one. Write those 'just beyond reach' goals down. When you create your list, remember that you have more capabilities, skill, and creativity than you give yourself credit for.

Focus on solving the 'almost impossible' and you'll continually impress yourself with how awesome you really are.

9 | PAY THE PRICE

"It is unreasonable to think we can earn rewards without being willing to pay their true price. It is always our choice whether or not we wish to pay the price for life's rewards."

- EPICTETUS

Everything has a price.

Want to win an Olympic gold medal? Become the president? Be a movie star? Own a farm? Write a book? Teach a cat to do a backflip?

That's great, and I admire your gumption. If your talents and passions indeed have their intersect in those places, then you can (and should!) accomplish those things.

The final key is the price tag. What does accomplishing your desire entail, exactly? What needs to happen before you stand on the gold-medalist's platform, swear in as president, see your name in the credits on the big screen, or do whatever the almost-impossible goal is, for you?

And then what? I mean, after those things happen, THEN what will be required of you?

What I'm asking you is… is this whole darn pursuit worth it to you? Are you willing to pay the price of getting to your goal?

It's okay to say, "no."

If it's not worth it, be at peace with that. You can't – and shouldn't – do everything there is to do on this planet. That's not your right as a human being. Besides, part of the key to being super-awesome is acting on what's worthwhile and ignoring what's not.

But if you say, 'yes' to the price, then by all means, pursue that lofty goal with no reservations, hesitations, or look-backs. Go for it with your whole self. You will start a journey of enormous growth.

If your own confidence is not enough for you, be encouraged in knowing that you have the blessing of The Great One.

An easy way to consider the cost is to think back to those three heroes of yours. You already know that you will reap their same life rewards if you make their same investment.

Therefore, when weighing the cost, consider if you truly want to *be like* that hero of yours. You may wish to SAY you've done what your hero has done, but a more useful approach is to ask if you want to BE who your hero IS after you've done what they have. That is the real cost of your pursuit.

If you're willing to pay the price, then with your whole self, pursue that thing. You'll be sitting on the rightful throne that belongs to your royalty within.

In other words, GO FOR IT.

Could you fail? Maybe. Might your face get smeared in the mud? It's possible. Is there a chance that you won't reach your goal. There is.

But there's also a chance you'll be super-awesome and crush it.

And if not, you'll be one step closer to the place you're *actually* going in life (even if it's not exactly where you think, right at this moment).

And EITHER WAY, it's not the success or failure that really matters . . . it's the growth. In growth is where you belong, you amazing human, you.

PART II

SUPER AWESOME PURPOSE

10 | OWN YOUR OWN SIGNIFICANCE

"Whether you try too hard to fit in or you try too hard to stand out, it is of equal consequence: you exhaust your significance."

CRISS JAMI

You are the captain of your ship and master of your soul.

Congratulations!

Gee, thanks. But what does that even mean?

It means that you are the owner of your own life's meaning. It means it's up to you to determine the significance of your life's events.

Mmmkay. Little more please?

For every life event, whether good or bad, your brain will attach some sort of meaning or significance to it.

Yep, your brain is up there in your skull, constantly trying to work out the meaning of the information it's receiving. It's trying to make sense of it all and explain how it all matters to YOU.

This task is one of your bodies processes that works like breathing. Your lungs work whether you're thinking about them or not, right?

Well, just like with each breath, sometimes your brain will assign shallow meaning or significance. Sometimes it will be deep and profound.

But you can also hijack your breathing, right? You can take charge of it, just by thinking about it and deciding that the next breath will be different. So you assign your lungs the task of taking a deep breath. Or you can force yourself to breathe quickly, shallow, slowly, or even to hold your breath.

The brain's override function works exactly the same when it comes to attaching significance to your life's events. Your brain will do it for you if you don't stop to think about it. Yet you can also hijack your significance-processing-center and decide that any given event actually has a profound significance. You can give any event a shallow meaning. You can even just decide that what happened isn't worth assigning any meaning to.

To be clear: you can choose to take control of how your brain interprets the significance of each of your life events. If you don't make it a conscious effort, your brain will create a significance all on it's own.

For example, what if you find yourself in some terrible circumstance? What if you're deeply hurt, mourning, or even feel like you can't put yourself back together?

I've been there. And I get it. It sucks. And I'm sorry. I can tell you that during the worst events of my life, they felt permanent and inescapable.

For me, therapy helped. It gave me a permission to feel, to mourn, to cry, and to sort out my jumbled thoughts.

During that inner work, I noticed a small bit of space emerged in my mind. I started to realize that it was my brain quietly asking the question, "how does this matter?"

Whenever you recognize those same subtle moments of space, and you're able to hear your brain asking that critical question, THAT is your moment to decide the significance of your life's events. That's when you get to choose, right then and there, the meaning and significance that these unwanted events will have on your life.

Like bubbles in a pond, you just have to stop long enough to watch them emerge. They will. In fact, you're probably having one of those moments right now as you think about that unresolved thing that you may or may not be thinking about.

You can change the meaning of that thing that happened. It may take some work, even in a professional setting, like it did for me. But you can give those awful life moments a empowering significance.

Holocaust survivor Victor Frankl, in his book, *A Man's Search for Meaning,* claims that those who found a meaning and a purpose in Auschwitz were those who had the best chance of survival. I understood him to be saying that in extreme cases, finding one's meaning and significance could be the difference between life and death.

We've all heard that "life is a gift." But have you ever considered that gifts are usually given when the giver wants to pass along something of value?

That's why I think that the greater power who gifted us our lives and this entire existence did so because your life, and our existence, is something of great value.

That's also why I believe that despite the most heart-wrenching and tragic of moments, it's our calling to decide upon more helpful, more empowering, and more uniting meanings of significance; meanings that are more aligned with a Greater Power's belief in the value of what you've been gifted.

You're created in the Giver's image, which means that you get to create your own meaning and significance. It's your choice. In my mind, that means there zero reason to choose *any significance* except for the best possible option.

So I implore you: find an empowering significance within each of your life-defining stories. Even the terrible ones. Define an empowering meaning and you will have joy, no matter how dire your situation.

11 | DON'T GIVE A RIP

"I couldn't care less what the colors are in reality."

-VINCENT VAN GOGH

Don't give a rip about others' opinions of your value.

Don't misunderstand; I'm not saying to stop caring about other people, or even to stop being curious about what they think. Just don't let their opinions about your value affect your own self-determined worth. In fact, if you let the voices and opinions of others determine your value, you are letting those people own you. Do that, and you're just giving away the keys to the kingdom.

Instead, choose for yourself what makes you valuable and worthwhile. What makes your life significant?

If you consciously answer that question, then your external circumstances will never be able to assess your value. Truth is, you own the deed to your house, and you were born clutching the receipt to your self-worth. You are the only one with the access code. You can give those things away if you choose (as many people do), but rightfully, they are yours.

YOU own your own significance. YOU define your own self-worth.

If you believe those are true sentences, then decide that's enough. Quit looking for excuses to give away the receipt and throw out the keys. Those belong to you!

Care for others and love them . . . but don't worry if they don't decide to do the same. That's only a reflection of their value and significance, *not yours*.

Do pay attention to their feedback. Search their reactions and accurately see what works foe you and what doesn't work. Hone in your focus how you can continue to grow, improve, and connect. But don't ever let someone else's opinion define your personal value.

Nah, don't give a rip about that.

A terrible fate would be that when you become old and withered and on your deathbed, you realize that you lived out someone else's life. But the worst fate of all would be to realize that you lived a life of desperately trying to meet your imagination's understanding of other people's expectations.

12 | SEE LIFE ACCURATELY

"The irony, though, is that that very desire for confidence is precisely what ends up undermining the accuracy of their decision."

-MALCOM GLADWELL

When you stub your toe, do you scream in your mind, "I'm an idiot!"? Or if someone honks in traffic, does your brain say, "that person must hate me! Arghhhhh!" If you get a grade below what you expected on your test, do you think, "now I'll *never* get into college"?

All of those are examples of not seeing life for what it is. All you did was stub your toe. The driver honked. You got a C on a test. End of story. That's it. Take a breath, relax, learn from those negative experiences and go on with your day. Reacting with anger, self-pity, or resentment (all code-words for lack of deep joy) are ways that we force inappropriate negative emotions onto our life events.

Next time you stub a toe, pretend you're watching a movie of yourself and laugh. Hear a car horn? Play them '*Jingle Bells*' with your own car horn. Get a bad grade? Take it as an signal and an opportunity to learn what you missed *and* as an opportunity to learn how to learn more effectively.

Feelings are the result of your opinions, not about factual matters. Life's events are not in your control. But your opinions ARE. So in order to feel better (aka: happy) change your opinions about the events that happen in your life. In turn, you will change your feelings.

At select times, this will mean that the correct action is to become MORE upset, outraged, furious, or defensive. Those are not bad reactions in and of themselves; it's the inappropriate use of those emotions that becomes problematic. At times, they are entirely appropriate.

Most people interpret events in terms of success or failure. "We won the game; we're winners." "I didn't get that sexy person's number; I failed."

This is the disease of closure-itis. It's the condition where we block out the more useful and creative interpretations.

Seeing life accurately would be to say, "we won. Let's celebrate . . . and figure out what we did correctly so that we can repeat it next game . . . and let's send footage of the game to talent scouts and universities . . . and let's be gracious winners because we know what it's like to be on the losing end as well."

Or, if something gives you a negative emotion:

OK, I didn't get that sexy human's number. What did I say (or not say) that didn't appeal? Could I have done anything differently to create a stronger connection? And actually, this means I've now got the time and the space available for someone who wants to reciprocate. That's very exciting! So thank you, random stranger for saying 'no' to me, because now I can freely meet someone worthy of my time and energy and my sexy soul.

Master this skill and you will find a hidden opportunity in all events, no matter how horrible or wonderful.

Seeing life accurately means having logical 'cause and effect' thinking.

If you're more skilled at any given, does that mean you're a superior human being? No. Of course not. That would be inaccurate thinking.

A definite "no-no" of accurate thinking is to assume your superiority due to a past accomplishment. Another is to fret about your what your imagination is telling you other people are thinking.

To think accurately means to accept reality, to take things at face value, not making illogical leaps.

Instead, be super-awesome and see things accurately, as they are.

13 | LIVE IN THE NOW

"Yesterday is history, tomorrow is a mystery, but today is a gift. That is why it is called present."

-MASTER OOGWAY (IN *KUNG FU PANDA*)

Live in the moment.

Life is not a dress rehearsal.

It's always showtime.

Choose the right character to be in the right now.

Be 'present' with the people who are around you.

Don't let your thoughts slip to the future, or the past, except at the correct times to do so.

I say these things because fears about the future won't affect it and regrets about the past won't change it. Just the same, hope for the future won't affect it and celebrations of the past won't change it, either.

Yes: prepare, dream, plan, learn, and celebrate. But don't waste precious energy and time on anxiety when you could be living in 'the now.' Use your emotional reserves to be integrated with what is around you, right now, in the present moment.

Have you ever wondered why societal anxiety spiked in tandem with cell phone technology? I believe it's because phones ask us to live in the future or in the past. Throw in heaps of comparison over other people's highlight reels, and it sends us reeling out of the present moment and into the future or the past.

Send a text. Wait. Somewhere in your brain, you worry about what they'll say. *Did my tone come across correctly? What will I say when they respond? What will I do if they respond differently to how I wish?* It becomes an endless open loop of future and past living. In other words, anxiety.

Or, if you post a photo.

What do you do next?

You wait. While waiting, you think, *should I really have posted that? Was it too much? Will anyone like it? Omigosh, look at how many people like it! How will my next post ever compete?*

Living too much in the past and the future is the source of most of our anxiety. It steals us from the present.

That's why, when someone is living in the 'here and now,' we say that that they 'have presence.' Because they are here. Not in their heads. They're present.

Here's the major problem with living in the future or the past: it makes deep joy conditional. We think, "I'll be happy when I get married, when I get a raise, when my mortgage is paid, when I've finished my exams, when the kids are through college, when I've put away enough for retirement . . ." And it never stops!

No matter our past regrets or future fears, no matter our past prides and future hopes, the result is always the same: rather than simply experiencing happiness, we end up looking for the next thing that falsely finishes the sentence, "I'll be happy when . . ."

This is a foolish approach because happiness is something to be had right now. In this moment. Regardless of the future or past or even your present circumstances, you can get a major bump in happiness by experiencing the moment more often. After all, joy is independent of time and can only be experienced in the 'now.'

Make the cold-blooded decision to create a happiness habit. Your joy doesn't depend on what happens or happened. Instead, if you will ever become happy, you must be happy. Period.

You will never be happy 'when' or 'of only.' If joy isn't practiced in the moment, then it is never experienced at all.

Don't assume celebrities, political leaders, TV show hosts, Instagram celebs, YouTubers, or wealthy business folk have happiness or a sense of meaning. Many are the worst 'living in the now' offenders around. After every project, campaign, episode, post, new subscriber, or new dollar earned, they start worrying about multiple other projects, never pausing to enjoy the fruit of their labor.

I know, because I am a serial offender.

But this story has always helped...

A wealthy, middle-aged businessman went on vacation to a tropical island in the South Pacific. He saw a fisherman who was a few years his younger, selling fish at a local market.

"You know," said the businessman, "if you went through years of business school, then hired many other fishermen, then opened a factory, you could distribute these fish all over the globe and become rich!"

"Then what?" the fisherman asked with a disinterested calm.

Sharply, as though insulted that the fisherman wasn't more excited by his ivy-league advice, the businessman answered, "well, so that one day you can live on a beach and enjoy time with your family, and go fishing."

Patient, the fisherman said, "But sir… I live on a beach. I spend time with my family. And go fishing each and every day."

They blinked and stared at one another for a moment. Then the businessman grumbled and walked away, his purchase in hand.

His vacation? Ruined! Not because of the fisherman's reply, but because he lives in the past and the future to too great a degree.

Meanwhile, the fisherman didn't think twice of the interaction. That day, he was too busy playing with his family on a beach to think about anything else.

He was too busy experiencing the moment.

14 | CHOOSE YOUR CHARACTER

"The adventure evoked a quality of his character that he didn't know he possessed."

- JOSEPH CAMPBELL

Each of our personalities has access to many 'characters.'

Within each of us lies a warrior and a peacekeeper, a parent and a child, a student and a teacher, a jester and a sage.

Some of our characters are gorgeous while some are ugly. Some kind, others cruel.

The skill is learning to choose the most appropriate character 'role' to play in each of life situation.

Take yourself out of reacting to each event and every word said to you. Instead, accurately evaluate the situation. Then, choose which is the most perfect character for this moment. Fully embody that avatar.

Do you see the profound nature of what I'm telling you? You have the privilege of being intentional. That means choosing, each day, each moment, who you will be.

You are the aggregate of your actions, not your imagination's idea of you that's floating around in your mind, about who you think you are. You are not your potential; you are your choices.

If you want to be a wonderful human being, then in each day, each moment, be intentional about embodying the character best suited take action on your current scenario.

A wise person develops the habit of instantly asking, in each situation, "Which is the most appropriate character for me to play, right now, in this moment?"

More specifically, is it time to be gruff or time to be tender? Time to stand up or time to stand down? Time to persist or time to quit? We all have these dichotomies within our capacity.

There's nothing unusual about the person who can move along these spectrums. Rather, super-awesomeness lies with the person who chooses the right character for each scene.

Generally, you want to ignore and shun your 'edgier' characters. Shunning the thief, the gossip, the destroyer, and the fighter are nearly always good ideas. Yet sometimes, these 'bad actors' deserve their screen time, too. In fact, there are moments when these are the only appropriate character selection.

For example, when wronged, be the thief; take back what's rightfully yours. When there's injustice, be the gossip; give voice to stories that share the truth.

The destroyer is needed for corruption and the fighter is needed for those who can't fend for themselves.

All of our inner characters have their appropriate time and place. None are good or bad in and of themselves, any more than the cloth of a puppet is benevolent or evil. Rather, it's you who chooses your virtue based on which character you select for each life event.

In each moment, choose wisely.

PART III

SUPER AWESOME TACTICS

15 | CHOOSE YOUR COMPANY

"When a person's character is not clear, look at their friends."

- JAPANESE PROVERB

Just as melted plastic assumes the shape of its mold. You, too, will assume the 'shape' of the people you spend the most time with. You choose your own mold by choosing your company.

Are your friends making you better? Are your associates? Are your family members? Or do they drag you down? Either way, by spending your time with them, you'll assume the shape of their characters. So be sure of your answer.

Be selective about who you allow as your friends, and when possible, your colleagues, and neighbors. The world is full of talented, encouraging, optimistic, and forward-thinking folk.

It's also full of annoying, vexatious, lazy, and pessimistic people. The key is to surround yourself with those who inspire and help you to choose your best character in each moment.

You wouldn't walk around barefoot on a floor full of broken glass and rusty nails, would you? Duh. No.

But if your mind is much more valuable than your foot, then why do you watch trashy shows and spend time with people who bring you down?

Don't just safeguard your mind. Build it up with intention. Join a team of positive people who, together, work towards something that excites you and is larger than what you could accomplish on your own. Become a part of something bigger than yourself.

16 | TEACH

"The word 'education' comes from the root e from ex, out, and duco, I lead. It means a leading out. To me education is a leading out of what is already there in the pupil's soul."

-MURIEL SPARK

Once you've learned a concept or skill, teach it. Don't be a greedy miser. Share.

Knowledge and skills are infinite once you treat them as such. Rather than being a 'taker,' give back just as it was given to you. Don't gain and hoard your knowledge. Spread it. You'll be amazed at how your own wisdom multiplies in the process.

Like a healthy lake, you need an inflow and an outflow. Otherwise? You'l become a swamp. You will fester.

In fact, by teaching, you re-enforce, in yourself, the very lessons you're passing along, therefore expanding your own knowledge during the process.

That's why Robert Heinlein said, "teaching is the highest form of understanding."

When teaching, be wary of students who think too highly of you, lest you lose your grasp on reality.

Don't inflate your head with self-importance or you'll poison the very students you're trying to help.

Teachers are not superior humans to their pupils, only advanced in knowledge and technique. You're no greater than anyone else, so help your students to become their best selves via the skills and information you're sharing. And while you and your students both make mistakes along the way, don't forget to play and forgive. That's how you grow, remember?

Inspire and teach, but know that the proof of a quality educator is when your students don't need to leech on you. True educators teach self-sufficiency, not dependence.

Good thing you're a rock star and are better than that. Keep slayin' it!

17 | LISTEN MORE THAN YOU TEACH

"Wisdom is the reward you get for a lifetime of listening when you'd have preferred to talk."

– DOUG LARSON

You're given two ears and one mouth.

Use them accordingly.

Besides, you already know all that you know.

If you only yap about all your super-awesome knowledge and stories, you'll have shut yourself off from learning. You'll stop growing. You'll cease to be super-awesome, and instead just be telling a bunch of stories about when you used to be cool.

Seek first to understand where other people are coming from. Do that by asking. Then, be present, shut up, and listen.

18 | PAMPER YOURSELF

"Talk to yourself like you would to someone you love."

- BRENÉ BROWN

For a massive boost in joy, give your body top-notch pampering.

These next four admonitions will sound basic but their collective result on your happiness is profound.

1. **Make exercise fun.** Find something that makes you *want* to get out and be active. Make your body move and you'll instantly think and feel better. If lifting weights in a gym is mind-numbing to you, then get out and run. If running bores you, join a team. Got butterfingers? Go surfing. Change it up until it feels like play to you.

2. **Eat clean.** Put stuff into your body that correctly fuels it. You wouldn't put vinegar

in your car's gas tank. So why do people fill their grocery store carts with blocks of cheese and chocolate, and packaged potato chips and sugary drinks (then grab a magazine at the checkout that says, "How to Feel Better and Get a Flatter Belly")? Take the time to learn which foods are the right 'gas' for your body, then eat those. I promise you, nothing tastes as good as healthy feels.

3. **Sleep like a baby.** You need 7-9 hours of sleep a night. You know this, so why do I still have to remind you? You will not function correctly unless you're well-rested. You'll look and feel like hell, then get wrinkled and everything will hurt. Make it a top priority to figure out how your body optimally rests.

4. **Get a massage.** It feels awesome, releases toxins, and helps prevent injuries. Get a foam roller or a electric massager if need be, but your body stores stress and it's good to physically work it out.

19 | BE DECISIVE

"The way to develop decisiveness is to start right where you are, with the very next question you face."

– NAPOLEON HILL

Don't dilly dally. Ain't nobody got time for that.

Make your decision. Eliminate all other possibilities. Scuttle your ships and take action towards your goals.

Say what needs to be said. Do what needs to be done. Don't second-guess yourself.

Say, "that's what's happening." Then do it.

PART IV

SUPER-AWESOME GOODBYES

20 | REJECT REJECTION

"I don't want anyone who doesn't want me."

— OPRAH WINFREY

If a child ran up to you and said, "you're a stupid carrot face!" you'd laugh. You know that the kid doesn't have enough information to pass a valid judgement. Plus, it's probably more about what's going on with the kid than you actually having... an orange vegetable face.

So why, when an adult insults you, or does something that irritates or hurts you, do you become offended when you know very well that what they've said isn't valid? Why don't you also tell yourself that their tantrum was probably more about what they're going through than anything you've actually done.

It's okay to determine that someone else doesn't have enough information to judge you with validity. If you've listened to what they're saying and considered it with accurate thinking, but still determine that their verbal rejection of you was wrong, then it doesn't merit any further worry any more than if a toddler called you a carrot face.

In other words, 'reject rejection.'

This has more useful applications in life than toddlers calling you vegetable heads. What would your life look like if you rejected the rejections of...

Breakups.

Job losses.

Not getting the job.

Bad interviews.

Not being accepted into a school.

Not being invited.

Not getting called back.

And so on.

If the criticism was invalid, then it's time to reject it. If you've determined that it's just not true about you, then decide that you're not going to waste another precious second worrying about how you can fix someone else's mistake or invalid criticism.

Reject the rejection and move on.

Stay open to acknowledging when you're wrong and when you're being made aware of one of your blind spots.

Especially if you seem to always go through the same mistreatment, with different people and events... usually means you're being a given a mirror with which to see yourself more accurately.

If that happens, don't be afraid to look in that mirror. After all, if more than three people independently call you a carrot-face, maybe it's time to take a look and see it for yourself.

21 | SET YOURSELF FREE

"Letting go means to come to the realization that some people are a part of your history, but not a part of your destiny."

STEVE MARABOLI

If you wish to be free, then don't worry about anything that is outside your 'circle of influence.' If you do, your emotions will always be a slave to your circumstances.

After you identify the things that are out of your control and you've decided that it's not worth the effort to put those things within your control, quit on them.

Yeah, quit. Let it go. You're free of that thing. Stop worrying about it. Stop hoping for it to change, stop wishing it was different. It's not. So just stop. Your well-being is affected because of something that isn't going to become different by your efforts. Why do you continue letting things you can't control ruin your valuable time?

Freedom is not just being free to say 'yes' to what you want, but it's equally about being free to say 'no' to what isn't good for you.

So say 'no' to more stuff. Literally, do not worry about it. By artfully and respectfully giving up on the attitudes, beliefs, and even the people who are detrimental, you'll become *more* free.

If you've found that something is outside your circle of influence and it's not worth the struggle to put it within your influence, give it to God (or the universe, providence, luck, or whatever your beliefs are).

Once you've 'given' it to something bigger than yourself, you'll be able to feel at peace with what you can't or won't change.

22 | MAKE GRATITUDE A HABIT

"Learn to be thankful for what you already have, while you pursue all that you want."

—JIM ROHN

What makes us wealthy? Gratitude.

No matter how much money you have, you will never be rich until you feel grateful (of course, you can have a lot of money and also feel grateful).

Gratitude is a habit that can be developed like any other. First, make it a conscious process. When you step out your front door in the morning, make the decision to *feel* what you're grateful for.

Once that decision becomes a regular thing, start doing it during your evening commute. Be thankful, even in the mundane.

Eventually, feeling gratitude will become an emotional habit. Just as depression and anger can be addictive feelings for people, so can gratitude become pleasantly addictive.

Feeling grateful in each moment is a key secret to feeling wealthy each day, consistently filled with deep joy.

If you'd like to become fabulously wealthy, throw in some compassion, generosity, selflessness, humility, love, and passion.

Shun the bitterness, selfishness, ego, resentment, and frustration in your relationships which will make you poor.

23 | FIGHT LIKE HELL

"If you're going through hell, keep going."

-WINSTON CHURCHILL

Boldly declare your life as your own. Have the courage to chase your dreams. And make 'em big while you're at it.

Stand up for yourself. Quit caring what other people think and don't take lip from anyone. Say what needs to be said.

Never start a fight; always finish one. Fight for those who can't fend for themselves. Know when to walk away.

Become deaf to naysayers and shun negative people. If criticism is valid, change. If not, ignore it and move on. Don't live by other people's standards; make your own standards and live by those. Fight for your right to be super awesome.

A half-hearted spirit has no power. A tentative heart leads to tentative outcomes. Commit! Fight like hell for the things, places, events, and especially the people who mean the most to you.

24 | MOVE ON

"Don't cry because it's over, smile because it happened."

- DR. SEUSS

Each of us is on our own journey, much like passengers on a train.

Eventually, each of us has to say, "this is my stop." And then, we part ways.

After a beat, those same 'exit' doors of your life become entrances. Space has been made for those new fellow travelers to join you for the next leg of your journey.

In life, just like with train travel, we rarely know another travelers' stop. Some people may only be with you for a short time. Then, it's their stop. It's their time to go a different direction.

Others may be sharing the journey with you for a good while, maybe even getting off at the same stops as you and sharing your connections.

Maybe they'll disembark sooner than you expected, but then you'll magically see them again on another journey, sometime in the future.

If you're lucky, a few may journey with you all the way towards your final destination.

Nobody's being rude or cruel by getting off at their stops. Usually, you weren't wronged or mistreated. They're just on their own journeys, too, and the time they shared with you has come to a close. They're going where they need to go, and you're going where you need to go, too.

For you and I, this is our stop. This is where we go in separate directions. I've said what I have to say about what it takes to live a super-awesome life.

I hope that you'll adopt these virtues as your life's aims, because when I happen to get a few of them right, I'm filled with deep joy; I wish that same sense of fulfillment for you.

I'll look forward to seeing your smile lines when you're old. Along with the sparkle in your eyes, that's all the proof I'll need to know that you made your life a great adventure that was filled with deep, genuine, super-awesome joy.

"KINDLY LEAVE YOUR SUPER-AWESOME REVIEW ON AMAZON!

IT MAY SOUNDS LIKE SOMETHING MINI, BUT IT MAKES A SUPER-AWESOME WORLD OF DIFFERENCE.

THANKS A MILLION!" – JB

SEE AND HEAR THESE CHAPTERS PERFORMED BY THE AUTHOR BY SEARCHING YOUTUBE FOR @johnbeede

FOR A FREE MASTERCLASS BY THE AUTHOR, VISIT

WWW.JOHNBEEDE.COM

THAT'S ALSO WHERE YOU'LL FIND JOHN BEEDE'S OTHER WORKS, INCLUDING BOOKS, AUDIOBOOKS, PODCASTS, VIDEOS, AND ONLINE COURSES.

www.ingramcontent.com/pod-product-compliance
Lightning Source LLC
LaVergne TN
LVHW091228080426
835509LV00009B/1207